Toward the Heliopause

Toward the Heliopause

Joan Michelson

Liverpool UK
www.madjockpublishers.com

Copyright © Joan Michelson 2007
Edition January 2008

All rights reserved

No part of this book may be reproduced, stored in a retrieval system or transmitted in any form or by any means without the prior written permission of the publishers.

A CIP catalogue record for this book is available from the British Library.

Published by Mad Jock Publishers
www.madjockpublishers.com

Printed by Intype Libra Ltd.

Designed by Rols Sperling and Joan Michelson
Author photograph © Murray Gintis

ISBN 978-1-906439-01-9

Acknowledgements

Acknowledgements are made to the editors of The Rialto (UK) for an earlier version of 'Heart', to Ambit, for 'The Last Week' and an earlier version of 'Second Christmas', The Bellevue Literary Review for 'The Next Week' and an earlier version of '28 November 98'; and for competition commendations and prizes: Barnet Arts Council Open Poetry Competition 2003 for 'Song of Stone', Manchester Cathedral Poetry Competition 2003 for 'Wife's Song', Coffee House Publishers Poetry Competition 2003 for an earlier version of 'Autumn Storm', Biscuit Publishing Ltd. Poetry Competition 2003 for six poems including 'The Last Week', and Poetic Matrix Press Competition Editor's Choice publication for chapbook collection, 2002, 'Letting in the Light'.

My special thanks to friends who helped with these poems and encouraged me to complete the volume, especially Andrea Carter Brown, partner in poetry since 2000, Nelica LaGro, Jacki Reason, Saul Reichlin, Marina Sanchez, Caroline Stone, Jan Fortune-Wood, Denise Mustafa and Giles Taylor. For writing residencies, I would like to express my gratitude to the Ragdale Foundation, the Virginia Center for the Creative Arts, the MacDowell Colony, Fundación Valparaiso, the Arvon Foundation, the Atlantic Center for the Arts, Ann and Preston Browning of Wellspring House, and to the University of Wolverhampton for research leave and Julie Evans, Print Services Unit. Last, but by no means least, I am grateful to Dahman Ladjassa, manager of Sable D'or Patisserie, London, and to his staff for their generous treatment of an 'in-house' writer.

The poems of Geoffrey Adkins are in draft form as found on his computer. The quotes introducing each section are from the posthumous collection, 'Retiring to the Coast', Limestone Publications, London, 2000.

to Jessica in whom the future lies

for Geoffrey who saw beyond

while still alive

CONTENTS

The Wife	3
Letting Go	4

I. Seizure

Seizure (Geoffrey Adkins)	7
The Last Week	8
The Last Haircut	10
Sleep	11
Blood Oranges	12
Lament	13

II. Satan

Letter from Satan (Geoffrey Adkins)	17
Last Night Poem	19
Ars Poetica	21
Message to Satan	22
You	23
Heirlooms	24
The Next Week	25
Breath	26
January 21st	27
Resurrection Day	28
Final Signature	29
Coats	30
October 5th	31
Autumn Storm	32
28 November 98	34
Second Christmas	35

III. Slates

Classification of Slates (Geoffrey Adkins)	41
Smoke	43
Commuters	44
Wife's Song	45
Song of Stone	46
Song for Sleep	47

IV. Extraterrestrials

Message from Extraterrestrials (Geoffrey Adkins)	51
Letter from an Earthling	53
Voyager	59
Therapy	60
The Heliopause	61
Cliff Walks	62
Heart	67
Threads	68

Toward the Heliopause

*And smile with me, if you can,
at the whole strange business.*

Geoffrey Adkins
'The Corner House'

The Wife

I thought that you had died. Were dead.
So I set off to find a house
for just us two, your wife and child.

I reached a village built on rock.
that faced a surging seething sea
and climbed past jumble to the top,

and found you there alive and flush
opening a door for me.
Come in, you said, *Come meet my love.*

You led me up a spiral stair
inside a tower made of stone
with slits for light. And it grew dark,

too dark to see your other wife.
But I could hear and feel her breathe.
And so, I said, *you've a new life.*

Then I was taken with the thought
that you had found the place we sought
when you and I shared dreams and talked.

But you – and I should have known
the soul that wanders finds a home –
wordless, returned me to the road.

Letting Go

You are not here.
You are never coming back.

I repeat this daily.
Impossible to learn.

Anniversaries arrive.
Post in your name.
A gift you might have sent.

Propped against your pillow,
I sit on our bed.

Here between my thighs
your feet used to winter.

Last night our daughter,
nearly grown,
slept on your side –

her bones like your bones,
long and lean and strong.

She dreamed she breathed her breath
into you. And here
you were. But then she woke

to find me holding her.
And then – a stir of air,

and then, and now, and now
the letting go.

I.
Seizure

I picture you in a kind of space.

Geoffrey Adkins
'After the Stroke'

Seizure
Geoffrey Adkins

I fell down on the grass.
My heart bumped and jolted.
Each heart beat collapsed on me
like a wall and crushed me.
Then the bulb smashed.

I lay on the topsoil.
I lay on the subsoil.
I went down to the earth's mantle.
I slurred and twisted
among hot glands of rock

and saw, way up,
on the flighty rim of the earth,
a man in a coat like mine,
a man with a life like mine,
who ran and danced a few paces,
then fell down on the grass.

The Last Week

On Sunday we went for coffee.
My leg in plaster
and on crutches, I went slowly.
I told you, *Go ahead*.

On the way I met the phys-ed teacher
who does yoga.
He had half an hour. *Good*,
I said, *Come meet Geoff.*

Next time I saw the phys-ed teacher
was the Thursday after.
I told him you were dead.
He looked at me. *But*

we just met. I said, *It happens.*
I didn't see him after that.
I heard he returned to Sydney
with the girl he met.

So we had coffee Sunday. Monday
my plaster cast came off.
A bus ride Tuesday. You angry at
standing room only.

Wednesday you had your hair cut.
Of Thursday, do I remember?
Yes. You gave your evening class a miss
and did some desk work.

Friday we went swimming,
the three of us together.
I was still counting lengths
when you left for work.

You called out, *Enjoy your shopping.*
Winter coats, I moaned. *See you.*
Half-past four we saw you.
Then we found your will

and the letter-poem from Satan
filed in your computer.
It was time-marked two a.m.
that Friday, your death day.

The Last Haircut

On Sunday morning we went out for coffee
at our regular, the smoky World Café.
As usual we saw the dressed up worshippers.

They gathered at Park Chapel, vanished
through heavy wooden doors and started singing.
We sorted out our week. Third week in your

new job and first time in the chair, you were
addressing Heads-of-Centre from London boroughs.
This was fixed for half past two on Friday.

I'd better get my hair cut, you said. I chanced
to pass the barber shop midday on Wednesday.
I saw you through sun-struck cars that dazzled;

and thought that you could see me. I watched you exit.
But you didn't cross the road to say hello,
or even wave. Instead you turned away

as if you heard a calling and you ran
as if possessed of something not quite you –
a boy again, late and hurrying home.

I didn't know what to think. I felt abandoned
strangely, as if you were beyond the real,
your body repossessed by God and chapel –

The true serpent, you once said. On Friday
in clothes like Sunday best, you departed.
You made the Meeting but not the one you'd mentioned.

Sleep

We were young. No one bothered
much with clothes. You tried a few
other girls before we met
but none passed the test you set:
what mattered was how you slept.

With me, you professed to rest.
So the marriage we grew into,
which failed so many other tests
and tested us until the last,
lasted until death.

So now, undressed and wrapped in sheets,
I move from bed to bed to couch
as if reproached by sleep itself.
I lie awake and watch the dark.
I watch a thousand things unseen.

And when the cat returns at dawn
and he curls up, I think of us
as once we slept. Then I could rest.

Blood Oranges

Returned that winter rifted with stress
and that long week with feral cats
so monstrous we felt cats cursed
the place we'd booked and our hard talk.

Never had Spain looked so drab
nor felt so cold, so grim, so wet.
The huge hotel with marble stairs.
housed only us – two tight-lipped guests.

We'd had ten okay-years but now –
no child. No child. The future stalled.
Through window glass like castle walls
the sea, a moat of metal, froze.

Facts were: you had a child and feared
your own repeats. But could I leave?
Then the oranges appeared –
blood oranges beneath the trees.

In Stoke-on-Trent, post-war, such fruit
was rare, a treat on Christmas Day.
I watched you suck and drip the juice.
Our Jess was born when autumn came.

Lament

And are you gone from me?
And are you dead?
Who loved me always
and now prefer the wind.

And is it spring
with an untimely frost?
And are the bushes sticks?
And berry-flowers dew?

And do I waking wake?
And is this ground the earth?
And do I breathe in smoke?
And is this wind?

Oh are you not alive?
Who loved me as your own
and gave me seasons
buttered with the sun.

II.
Satan

*I heard a calmer version
of the verdict.*

Geoffrey Adkins
'To Visit a London Heart Specialist'

Letter from Satan
Geoffrey Adkins

Easier in the old days. Warrior dies. His spirit flies
to its ancestral home. Poets sing their lays.
In those days we just waved them through.
Hell, I should tell you, right off, is not
in the punishment business. Our chief activity
is record-keeping, we're all qualified
accountants and information theorists.

Our job is to register death, to record
the final, finest fractioned sensations
of departure. Our records are computerised
and precisely edited. Not a single sparrow falls
etc, no leaf wanders to the grass
– you know the rest from Sunday School.
And frankly, the chief problem we face
is the appalling forgetfulness of human beings,
the vastness of what you do not wish to know.

It stands to reason that hell is not the afterlife
if such a place exists. Our interest is
in the transition from life to its other.
Translating the image to its reverse.

The rules which god has organised
are simple but crude. All of life, he said,
and all of afterlife belong to me. Your domain
is the transition. Wafer-thin moment
between two huge continents. Edge of a sheet
of paper. Thinner yet – as thin as the width
of a single cell. Thinner yet, the envelope
of non-existence which contains a thought.

Or, if you like, think of us as border police.
So, we police the transition. Crude. Everybody
knows this. Jesus himself, and the prophets
had a good inkling. But even they were not
exempt. They too, screaming and struggling,
have to pass through our interrogation.

And is this so terrible? Would you prefer
to give up all this torrential experience
for life in a narcotic daze? I think not.
And this is why we're on the side of the poets.
One day, some day you'll come over
to our side of the fence, and join our banner.
They all do, eventually. You see they cannot bear
a death, are not equipped for it.

Each person labours up the staircase entirely alone,
some jauntily, some gasping with angina.
Every fragrance will be returned to you,
every smallest triumph. It's a good deal.
No catch.

Last Night Poem 'Letter From Satan'

On the last night you sat up late working
from half-past ten. You wrote meeting notes,
revised your will – that time of year – this time
including B, your brother. After midnight
you updated Satan's letter, a poem with
cunning winning words that try my understanding.

Two a.m. I heard you in the garden.
You were rustling up the fox, the vixen,
the one you used to feed. She's mangy now
with a new cub that's blind. (Glad you can't see.)
You'd look for her and look for stars. No stars
that night nor vixen. Still you had your pipe
and lingered for the pleasure of the hour.

With pleasure too you stripped for bed and slept.
In the morning, everything on schedule.
You joined us for our swim. We saw Jess off.
Your turn to drive to school mid-day. You drove,
collected Jess – with bicycle and flute,
made lunch and one last time you tsk'd, 'You'll give
yourself an ulcer, sweetie, eating hunched.'

You had an ulcer. And confessed to Jess
a pang from 'gulping down' your breakfast bagel.
All clear, you disappeared to pack your bag
with papers for the meeting you were to chair.
You had an hour. I've told and told this part.
You left late. You hurried towards the train,
climbed up and down the station steps and fell.

A man can do so much and nothing more.
The night before you edited your will
and reworked your letter-poem from your
Mister Satan, Director-Manager-of-Data.
The poem seems to justify the desk-bound
record keeping that we poets do.
Hell's not so bad, you wrote, *no worse than earth*.

Facts: Hours from death you pictured this:
A man like you – entirely alone.
He's gasping, labouring up the station stairs.
Or he's so crazed with promise of returns
from Satan speaking through your letter-poem –
despite his failing heart and the ascent,
his step is jaunty and he goes up fast.

At two pm you died on Hornsey Station.
Waiting for your train. On platform one,
the over ground North London line to Moorgate.
A mild and milky afternoon. The driver
rang from his compartment. As if alive,
you were sent by ambulance to hospital.
British Rail informed the Tottenham Police.

Listen to me one more time. How can you
write to us, *Is this so terrible?*
Your departure is – terrible.
How can you offer us *returns of triumphs?*
Insist you're on our side. *Good deal. No catch.*
And leave me here assigned to be your widow
and your record-keeper. For weeks I wrote

next to nothing. I've found in pencilled scribble
the number left to call Police Control;
one word beneath it – barely legible –
gutted. About the hours of disbelief,
slow-motion steps, the way time emptied
into space that froze and my body
moved obediently without me, not a word.

Ars Poetica

Ghosting Satan, you left a letter-poem
addressed to us about record keeping
and forgetfulness in human kind.

You warned us firmly as you listed rules.
*Pay attention to sensation. Be precise
in your descriptions. Honour fact.*

I'm reading these and thinking of my mother's
rules. She spoke them. *Tell it as it was.
Portray us as we are with feet of clay.*

From Horace we have 'Ars Poetica' with do's
and don'ts. Archibald MacLeish continued
this tradition, *Being and not meaning.*

Okay, I say. *Okay. But what about
the heart?*

Message to Satan

Seven times in seven years, I've drafted
a reply to you and hit 'delete'.

Am I angry still? Still baffled?
Why did you speak for Geoffrey his last night?

I'd like to shake you, Satan, until your bones
are fit for nothing but an stock-pot.

Go on gloating. Clerks like me and my dead
husband helplessly obey an urge

to write. Everything goes down on paper,
or computer. We file, read, rewrite.

Again I read your letter. I want an answer.
Must I accept no answer? Your phone

does not connect. It's my receiver I hear
humming crassly. I watch it hit the bed.

You

We found you on a gurney by a window
dressed for work and rumpled from your fall.
You wore your father Jim's grey trousers,
the unworn polyester you'd found and claimed
when we had cleared his house two years before.

I'm reading 'Jim', the poem that you wrote
about his dying. *I missed it by one day.*
I wept into my hands despite being
over fifty. The ambulance had stood
outside the house half an hour as they tried

resuscitation. I imagine a similar
scenario for you – medics squatting
on the Hornsey platform half an hour.
Policemen drove us to the morgue at Middlesex.
Yes, it was you lying there –

your pale eyes empty. I fell on you
and felt a chill, a spear of ice that reached
from end to end and numbed. Then – strange sounds.
They seemed to come from nowhere but were mine.
Enough, I told myself. *Enough. Enough.*

I stood up, walked out, signed that you were
Geoffrey Graham Adkins, son of Jim.
With Jess behind me, I followed the policemen,
a couple – young – to the car. On Monday
they came round with your father's watch.

Heirlooms

There is no last goodbye but a last touch
and then a final look or glance that lives

inside the future. *A prince*, you wrote of Jim
when you saw him readied for the fire.

A prince, we write of you, our magic prince
to kiss awake or kiss for a long sleep

and a forgetting. So we found the building where
they checked you out, confirming *ischmaemic*

ventricular. And I signed the form.
Never mind. We were expecting 'heart'.

There was time (we had forever) to whisper
some last words, to leave a special letter

and to cut some of your greying hair.
But not accepted by the coroner.

He was concerned about his handiwork.
We'll take care of it. Please wait here.

He took our letter, scissors and our envelope
and left us staring through your cage of glass.

The hair is in the drawer with snips of mine.
And there your father's watch, your specs, a pen

and even after years, the smell and taste
of burnt tobacco wedged inside your pipe.

The Next Week

The next week vanished, though there
were days, and each asked something

beyond mourning with the mirrors
covered, since nothing was prepared.

On Monday you were autopsied.
On Tuesday booked for burial

in a double-plot we bought
in Enfield. On Wednesday the search

for clothes to wear and answering
the phone. Thursday, half-past three,

the ceremony. Then we tried
to cover up your coffin using

one shovel made of iron
and our hands. Was there a Friday?

On Friday you were one week dead.
I remember warmth on Sunday.

My sister packed her bag, then walked
with us through Highgate to the Heath.

Breath

You edge out into the cooling aftermath
      Geoffrey Adkins,
      'After the Stroke'

Through the window of the local Y
where we breathe in rhythm with our yogi,
I hear a train speed past.

I see you fallen but I go on breathing –
out with force, then feeling air flow in –
which fortifies the heart.

We're told Tibetan Buddhists practise naked,
cold in snow until their bodies itch
and sweat with fire, and glow.

I breathe out *shoo-ooo-ooh-ooo-ooh* for grief
and hold in emptiness until the dust motes
and the window tremble.

Rise all the way on breath and breathe, we're told.
I see you – arms uplifted to the purer air.

January 21st

They say I fell because you fell.
First day back at work, I missed the kerb,
landed on my face, broke my glasses,
gashed my cheek and lip. A colleague rushed me

to Emergency. There I finished
filling in the form for your bronze plaque
with words that Jess and I agreed felt right:
Father Lifemate Teacher Poet.

I added up the cost, wrote a cheque,
then dozed until my name was called. I saw
a doctor who looked about as old as Jess.
Ultra-cautious, he took his time deciding

he'd better open up the wound to clean it
before stitching. He warned that it would hurt.
I shrugged. I wasn't worried about pain.
Since you'd been gone, my body had felt distanced

as if re-housed inside a carapace.
I think he could have nailed me up and pierced
my fingers. Would I have felt even that?
He left a scar, my own stigmata,

a ridge of Braille that paled with time and turned
from pink to white. When I visit you
and for a moment rest against your plaque,
my face feels cool but my left cheek burns.

Resurrection Day

For weeks I'd watched the grass grow long,
reproached myself, and let it go on growing
as if by miracle you might return.

Finally, on Easter Sunday, I took control.
I found the shed key, lifted out the Flymo,
unwound the orange cord and cleared the stones.

Mowing, I stopped repeatedly to move
the cord. Grass cut, I put the mower back.
I know you would have done much more – cleaned

the blades, raked the cuttings, trimmed the beds
and edges of the paths. Then tea in hand
you would have walked around surveying all.

But I lay down and closed my eyes to breathe in
grass and earth. I wanted only that.
But instantly I saw you in your coffin

being lifted towards me. On your back.
A sheet pulled to your neck. Your skin clay-brown
but quickly changing colour as if, like mine,

your heart was pumping. Then I felt everything –
grass and earth but also hair and skin,
the wrinkling around your eyes, the roughness

where you'd shaved, your nose, your jutting chin.
For warmth I'd dressed in layers. Your fleece was zipped
over mine. Your gardening gloves hugged mine.

My socks inside your socks inside my boots.
I pictured step by step undressing us
until we lay naked and I trembled.

Final Signature

Last date to settle the estate, June 5th.
I had to testify. *Is this the true
signature of Geoffrey Graham Adkins?*

The lines in your familiar script beat
like bony wings. I felt them through my skin.
But I was done with these imposing forms.

I could go home. Here engrained in tiles,
in honey cork you'd laid, another signature –
in black with gouged out circles like small eyes

from days when in the guise of guide you led
a cycling course for Jess age five. You peddled
through the kitchen door, past counters, sink,

the cooker and the thick-legged old pine table.
Matador, you raised a crumpled handkerchief,
and turning, waved, *Come on, our duck. Hup-hup.*

Hard-stuck garden pebbles scratched and gouged
the cork engraving it. Here – the evidence.
I scrub the floor until this writing shows.

Coats

*The money's on the table. Buy long winter
coats.* This was your last request
as if you saw the winter like no other –

girl and mother wrapped around each other.
The avalanche of agitation. You.
Not. Here. For weeks we couldn't keep warm.

New Oxford Street that Friday afternoon.
Not knowing and not buying. We found
the coats in June, with hoods, at half the cost.

October 5th

Before you left, you sawed the overhanging
eucalyptus which had grown wildly
into the neighbour's sun. You cut the grass,
weeded the packed beds beside the path,
and booked a trash collection with the Council
for stuff that's catalogued as special. More –
you purchased cable television, a new
policy for auto accidents,
a down jacket, boots, for Jess a piccolo,
and, forgetful, stamps for Christmas twice.

We used the stamps for the announcement. No
Christmas cards from us. A New Year's storm
smashed the porch roof you laid. The grass,
although I do your jobs, is deep again.
Now seeding. As for the stray you hosed and chased,
the feral tom, he climbed through the window
and sprayed our bed. The bed is gone. And summer.
I'm writing on the day we last pitched the tent
and camped in Suffolk, the only campers
in the dunes. All night the wind raged.

Autumn Storm

Tonight, another birthday for our Jess,
we turn the clocks back against the dark.

Like you when young, and because you're gone,
she is wandering the world. For both of us

I think of her first hours when we were three
together. You lifted her to count her limbs

and I looked up and saw her eyes were yours.
Today I crossed the Heath in winds that stripped

the oaks. At once the autumn went. It stormed
like this the day you brought us home.

Fretting about drafts, you stuffed the cracks
with paper wads and socks and wrapped us in too

many blankets. It was winter then,
so we stayed in – both of us – obsessed.

I held her, breast-fed, wrote, cooked, dressed –
all single-handed. When she woke at night,

you picked her up and paced, sharing secrets.
You showed her your beloved Pollack print,

an action painting with pooling spidery lines.
You talked about felicities of chance –

smearing, dripping, throwing. What am I mourning?
The craziness? The bliss? Your lost whispers?

When I'd been stitched and my placenta caught,
I was taken to a ward and ordered not to move.

Jess was snatched away. What happened after that
was wild and transcendent. Behind my eyes

a swirling light took off. It burst through glass.
to forge a universe – unknown, enticing, vast.
.

28 November 98

Eight days before you died, looking out,
you watched me from the kitchen window. I limped
towards you with my leg in heavy plaster.

As I came close, teasing me, you grinned.
And you kicked up and waggled your long floppy
bedroom slipper. I vanished round the corner,

came through the kitchen door and stopped beside you.
We both looked out. It was another grey
November twenty eighth, but not like this one.

Eight days to mark the circle of the year,
a noose that stops the flow. Day by day
pulled back, all past, time will not move.

Tonight it's dark enough to see a face
reflected in the kitchen window – my face.
Yet I see yours, and grinning. You can't be flesh.

A ring of hair, a pipe of cherry wood.
perhaps, long bones. Life that eats us up.
Where are we? The countdown to the fifth.

Second Christmas

i

Jess returned to London in November.
Her plan? To waitress through the holiday,
then find a job on a kibbutz. For Christmas
we stayed here. Christmas Eve, I visited

our waitress. Hair up, apron-ed, gracious, Jess
was glad to serve her 'mama'. She fed me well.
Home, I saw she'd left a spread of photos
on the table. I glanced at us. But no –

not for me. Easier to think about
the 'Rescue Service.' What if no one came
to fix the car? Jess was adamant.
Christmas Day we have to visit Daddy.

ii

She didn't get home till after two. But eight a.m.
she was knocking on the bedroom door
ready. Barely dawn. Frost overnight.
Cold. The heating not yet clicking on.

Come on, sweetie, slip in. There's lots of room.
In a minute I'll fetch tea and presents.
Jess wanted none of our traditions. And not
our Christmas morning trip to Highgate Pond

for the century-old swim meet with fire
crackling in a metal trash bin, hot mull,
mince pies, cake, announcements through a bull horn.
And she had second thoughts about our tree.

iii

We reached the cemetery far too early.
We sat and watched the wipers rise and fall.
At ten the park attendant let us in.
I saw you then, standing, come to greet us.

Just as fast the image vanished. We reached
your grave – bare earth with a stick marker.
I heard Jess whisper, *Happy Christmas Daddy*.
I felt I could bear anything but this.

At half-past ten the bugle always called
for swimmers. I could see you on the dock,
my towel and fleece bunched against your arm.
You always cheered as I jumped in and swam.

iv

Then for moments - sun. A sheen on grass
and plaques, those well set in and worn with years
and yours, the new ones cut this winter and placed
on mounds of earth for planting in the spring.

All bronze (the rule), rain-washed, they caught the light.
In sun I felt your name inflame me. I crouched
and saw your letters glow. I read them
cut by cut – your names, the dates, the words

we chose to put there. I touched the water mixed
with pebbly grit and twigs, some fine as hair.
I raised my finger and tasted only water.
Then I read and mouthed your name again.

GEOFFREY GRAHAM ADKINS
15 MAY 1941 – 5 DECEMBER 1997.
FATHER LIFEMATE TEACHER POET

v

After that, hoods up, getting wet,
reluctantly we started back. We passed
the older section from the nineteen sixties.
There the plaques were settled down in rows

orderly as graves for soldiers. We met
Harry Eakins near the exit. A bench
'for mom and dad', dead thirteen years. He'd brought
his tea – a large thermos flask and a box

of thick bread 'sarnies' - cheese - the way you would
for afternoons at the allotment. You two,
Eakins-Adkins mates, would have 'mooched' about
and poked through hedges at land still pastoral England.

vi

I like to think of you and Harry there
putting things to right. You would have helped him
with his bench. He would have helped you finish off
your plot – set the plaque and plant new grass.

I see you two sniffing round the skip
that over flows with tossed out flowering plants.
You'd rescue and recycle, plot more projects.
Only when the light was truly gone

would you turn home. You'd have your snug to keep you
warm – your desk, your Macintosh computer,
your pipe and (why not?) a bottle of your
home-made 'plonk'. Then you could write all night.

vii

Dinner with neighbours. Salmon. Sherry. Television.
Ten years had passed since Lockerbie. A memorial
with film of live footage from the crash.
A blur of silver-white flashes, last signs

of those many young college kids returning
home for Christmas. They died again on film
and in our minds. Then, live, we were shown snow
lighting on the gravestone that holds their names.

The mourners slow-walked past. Most just glanced.
But one, caught on camera, stopped, took off
a glove, and with one finger traced the letters.
Bells rang out in Lockerbie and London.

III.
Slates

*Let's take this lantern by its handle
and go indoors. Your mother's lighted window
does look inviting.*

*Let's leave winter outside, just the three of us.
See, I'll carry you in,
in my arms.*

Geoffrey Adkins
'Digging at Night'

Classification of Slates
Geoffrey Adkins

In a fervour of homemaking
we ordered classic slates for the roof.
We painted orange and blue panels in the bathroom,
purchased an old mahogany table from the auction –
ideal for dancing on.

We had a cathedral at the end of our street
looming above the cottages like a mother hen,
bells clucking us out of sleep on Sunday mornings
sending us off to the park at Verulamium
next to the city walls which Boudicca burnt.

Every step of the way was a history tour.
We wandered down to the Roman museum,
where a paw print is embalmed in mortar,
2,000 years old, which our dog Mortimer,
wiser than I was, sniffed at and moved on

in favour of the sexy and compulsive
fragrances of the present – a gift for the here and now
that dog had, which still I haven't achieved.
I believed then that history was alive; and easily
with each footstep I could shake up the flare

of a medieval head-dress,
or invoke those cathedral masons, in Everyman tunics,
clinging to their rickety elm-pole scaffolding,
as they cried 'send up' in Saxon or Norman
to the train of rubble-filled oxcarts

grating past our front door,
each with a different, elliptical grind and squeak
from the worn axle. For a new husband,
I was too fanciful. Too many ancient
and promiscuous companions

for the good of our marriage.
Too many echoes at dusk.
I was besotted with our ghostly neighbours,
but you yourself, with your mild
and discriminating passion, I turned away from

and forgot. And forgot that all the passions
of the past, compared with you, are nothing.
And then the premonitions of collapse.
The flooding along the Ver river at Christmas,
the bloodied partridges and pheasants;

the lanterns, and the wild faces of the game dealers.
It seemed that all of happiness would come down,
and so it did, and so it buried me, in the dust
and stillness of departure, a living city
deconstructed to a few bits of city wall

protruding through the turf like broken molars.
And when, at last, the cathedral roofer came,
with samples of slate tiles,
various oblongs, subtle and complicated
in their hue and texture, each separate shape

graced with a designation of its own
such as Princess, Marquessa, Queen,
I had to explain to him,
'My friend, you're too late. I have no house
to live in now, and no roof to mend.'

Smoke

Your shadow inhabits less,
though here you live, owner in name,
your scrawl on a thousand scraps.

Our lifetime of things goes on speaking,
the singing goes on broken and flowing,
the waters too. Unbridled, undaunted,

body and shadow fuse
Even, sometimes, the scent lifts
like smoke from bone.

Commuters

Your day-pack heavy on my shoulders
I leave the house with you and walk
quickly towards the train. Always
it is Friday, a bright winter
afternoon, the day you missed
the meeting and the message system
overloaded, leaving us
wondering where you'd gone.

You always walked a little faster.
I push my pace. I don't want
to miss my meeting either. But when
we reach the steps, I'm out.
The hare is you, taking steps
in leaps by twos and threes and fours
as if you're born again and Life
is calling. I'm the tortoise.

I crawl through litter step-by-step,
up the hard-pack edged with iron.
I count forty one, then cross
the bridge and count again. You call,
See you later, love. I see you later.
As my train pulls in, your pack
hits the siding and collapses
flattening on the track.

Wife's Song

I was taken to a room
with a man I did not know
and put to bed and tucked up tight.

A girl looked in, and seeing you
instead of him, said, *Wonderful.*
How wonderful. A miracle.

But then I found him in our bed.
I rose above him and I said,
I'm with the dead. Do what you like.

I thought you were completely gone.
But now you robbed me of myself.
And stole what I had saved to keep.

A naked man who looked like you
lay in our bed to take your place.
And what was I, my love, to do?

And then the house was set on fire
and I was told to walk away
and not look back. But I looked back.

Song of Stone

It was bold day but forest-dark
and black with boulders in the room
and through the bed where I conceived
trees and stones alike had grown.

Or rather stones like trees-in-stone
growing as if nursed by stone.
The branches pushed the windows out.
The ceiling lifted and sailed off.

There we lay like royalty
of stone, in stone, with human form.
On my left side, a cat in stone.
Overhead a gilded dome.

Until I woke and left the room
and wandered through the house alone.
The loft was stuffed with things entombed.
I understood that gone was gone.

Song for Sleep

I sleep and hold your hand
and hold your hand in sleep.

And there the moon slides in.
The eucalyptus breathes.
The garden shed grows tall,
taller than the hedge.

And years roll on, roll on
until we have no years.
Then, like blossom, floats
an alphabet of dust.

I hold in sleep your hand.
In sleep I hold your hand.

IV.
Extraterrestrials

*Millions of messages,
dense and silent, switching across time
call in my former selves.*

Geoffrey Adkins
'The Pedestrian Crossing'

Message from Extraterrestrials
Geoffrey Adkins

Earthlings, we have chosen to make contact.
Do listen carefully. We consider that you
are in danger. You remind us of a toddler
who has clambered on an unstable chair.
If he/she forgets him/her self for one moment

he/she will tumble down and split his/her
head open, or worse. Yours is a most vengeful
and tribal species unable to think clearly
because your minds are preoccupied
with reprisals – a vile thing for us to observe.

We think you should forgo
all nuclear weapons and similar.
On our future screens we have been receiving
lurid pictures of your Armageddon.
All the pages of your past will ignite
in one simultaneous blaze. The burning

of the library at Alexandria and all
the subsequent doleful catastrophes and mishaps
which you have brought upon your wretched selves
will be as nothing in comparison. The upshot

will be an embarrassed darkness, a bucket of ashes
in which the sole survivor will write,
'It wasn't my fault.'
All good entertainment, from this distance,
but not acceptable behaviour in a shared universe.

You can't stop children taking risks –
we know that from our own infancy – but we do insist
on much firmer parental control.
And that's why we've decided to adopt you,
every single one of you. We're intending

to take control of your minds until
you're more experienced and can safely
be given the key to the universe.
It won't hurt, just a few simple rules
which you must follow to the letter.
Goodbye for now. Expect

further communications. You'll know us
by our characteristic signature tune,
which you must all learn to hum.
And in the meantime, a note of caution.
We have reason to believe you

will be receiving other applications
for surrogacy from elsewhere. They'll come
in flattering and delightful forms
but you must shun them like the devil.
They mean you nothing but harm.

Letter from an Earthling

i.

Five years. I go on talking to you. Much
has stayed the same. Problems with the house.
The boiler went. A chimney sprang a leak

and leaked unnoticed until Jess returned –
flew in with barely time to pack for Bristol.
But you don't know that she accepted Bristol.

This coming June, she earns her honours. And then?
She'll leave the country. Once you weren't here, she lasted
only through exams. A-levels done – off.

Her room remains, her files stored like yours.
She framed and hung your poem for her,
'Career Advice from My Daughter'.

You used to be the Principal of a college
and that was passable although it meant long hours
and often you were late collecting me from school.

Then you announced that all along you'd really been
a poet. Well I hadn't noticed. And now you propose
to become a postman instead. I think you could do better.

Not a pss-chi-atrist because you'd be too impatient
with the patients, but what about a potter
or a pastry cook or a pied piper.

I wouldn't even mind if you become
an ordinary papa. I think I could
quite easily – with my driving lessons

just about to start and those essays that need
typing plus laundry and shopping for my
lo-cal nuggets – make that a fulltime job.

*You could still be a poet if you really wanted,
on a part-time basis say on Sunday afternoon,
from three o'clock to quarter to four*

*or when I'm away on holiday abroad,
as I intend to be, from now on quite often,
if you could just let me have the airfare please.*

ii.

Jess was sixteen then. Eighteen, she found
a job as dining room assistant at Interlochen,
the music camp in northern Michigan and needed

airfare. Then she travelled. Six months later –
home to sort things out. Then another airfare,
London-Tel Aviv – for a kibbutz-ulpan,

the plan from age fourteen that you'd approved.
20 hours a week of Hebrew classes, 20 hours
work for the kibbutz. First job, the worst,

the laundry. Next, dawn shift, field hut chef.
Toilet cleaner. Pool guard/cleaner. Translator –
Russian-Hebrew-English. She has your ear.

Turning twenty, she returned for 'uni',
angry that I made her. Endless issues.
Four years of bureaucratic battles.

Twice a subject change. Then restricting
her degree to Single Honours. Next adding Czech.
Required year abroad, she divided up

her residency between Russia and Israel.
Another air fare, this impromptu and one way
Moscow – Tel Aviv via Vienna. She found

a job as *madrichah* for new immigrants.
By email, she talked her Bristol tutor round
to crediting it and approving Russian-Israel

for her thesis topic. Then by telephone
she called on me, – this time, a little weepy,
You have to come. A very long weekend

in winter rain trapped in the Absorption Centre.
It was a tower block in the north
in an Arab village and filled with new Israelis.

They were student age and on their own,
mainly Russians but also some from Ethiopia.
Jess, on call, kept trying to keep things calm.

iii

You wouldn't believe what's happened to the world.
Especially since two thousand. I didn't forget
the New Year's walk we planned to do together,

Waterloo to Tower Bridge. You'd expect
the litter and the rowdy stragglers and murk
but not broken glass around the benches

and on the path, a tide of mean-edged shards.
One year later in Manhattan, departing
Boston planes were hijacked by new martyrs.

They hit the World Trade Centre – north, then south.
Both towers collapsed with whirlwind speed.
Since then, we've upped surveillance and have A War

on Terrorism. Our leaders, Blair and Bush,
(Bush Junior, President) are conspiring,
or so we're told, to bomb Baghdad this year.

Pre-war, we're out to stop this crazy war.
Remember Vietnam? March nineteen sixty eight.
The march to Grovesner Square. You were there.

*Hey, hey LBJ, how many
kids have you killed today?* And now? *Peace-
Shalom-Salaam. Not Our Blood For Oil.*

iv.

As for my job? Like you – made redundant.
Took my teachers' pension. I too feel more
relieved than shaken – although I miss my colleagues

and especially the students. Writing more.
Won a writing fellowship to Bavaria.
Special – but being there was not easy.

I felt your presence sharply. I kept seeing you –
stick in hand, tweed cap, specs off 'and dangling'
so you could read the map. I could have used

your expertise and your German. Each day
I walked an hour to reach a lake. Spring-fed,
the water in it pure enough to drink,

un-peopled, but marked with rustic lettered signs.
I understood. It was private. Yet daily
I stole in and swam the length. One day

late, I saw the naked sun draw a ladder
up and up from the bottom to slide
across the surface. The sides dissolved.

The rungs, free in space and silvery-gold,
continued climbing until they reached the sun.
They blazed. Then I heard you saying something

but of course you weren't. Then I was caught
by a sudden storm – lightning, thunder, rain.
I ran through such acreage of peas

in flower – thick and tall and tangled, I was
lost and felt the wonders turned against me.
Forest, rolling hills, lakes, these tracts

of land met facts I'd learned. For centuries
Jews with Germans, as Germans, were alive.
Here they lived. Yet I saw no sign. And none

of their removal sixty years ago.
The town memorial is gone. Remains?
Transferred elsewhere. A perfected cleansing.

For relaxation we have feudal-style
battles. Horsemen gallop up the hills
brandishing new wooden swords. On Saints' Days

church processions through the village with ancient
gilded icons carried carefully high.
Afterwards, in the square, an outdoor meal.

Beer, potatoes, schnitzel, oozing cream cakes.
Meanwhile your friend Ted, and only weeks
after publishing your last poems, 'Retiring to the Coast',

suddenly died like you of heart collapse.
On the public front, war is smouldering
in the Near East. Recently some women

and mostly young, many students, have worn
explosive belts, climbed on crowded buses
and killed themselves to kill many others.

v.

Is this my news for you? Your desk is still
stuffed with letters you had treasured – from friends
and us – Jess from pre-school onward, a card

from me I tucked between the bed sheets thirty
years ago. The nineteen seventies. We were
in our twenties. I'm sixty now, officially

a pensioner. Jess who does her hair
– keeps changing colour – urges me to highlight mine.
I should look younger. As for career advice?

I'm to find a job in London and keep it.
I can be a papa-style poet on Sunday morning
if I don't yell at her to go away

because I'm trying to write. Most important –
like my mother's mother from a muddy *stetl*
beyond Vilna, I'm to be a *Polonia*,

an *Old World Mother*. It doesn't seem to mean
Jewish so much as religiously devoted
to being *Ma*. When Jess is here – clean and cook,

lay a Sabbath table, light Sabbath candles.
When she's away, how I spend my days
is my affair. What's paramount is, *Stay stable*.

Stay at home so she feels free to travel.
No need to mention airfare. It's understood
Ma Polonia is good at business. She provides.

Here's a card Jess sent from Baja, Mexico
and one you sent from home to home when I turned
forty-one. That post card of the neon sign

from Hornsey Baths and Laundry: a woman diving.
Towards the next forty-one, you wrote,
I could even be a witness.

Voyager

The car was vast, a wooden room.
There we were condemned to march
pressed so close I felt my breath
slipping down your back like sweat.

And when you dropped, I felt the rise
of glacial-cold formaldehyde.
Next, the room became a box.
An opened flap – I was tipped out.

I crouched on earth, a raft in space,
to watch you, coffined, cross the sun
and, spinning, rise beyond the rim
into the dark. I woke – my throat

so parched and raw – I could not speak.
For weeks I watched this scene repeat.

Therapy

Each time she rang the bell, I was shaken.
She might have been a witch or an archangel
like your Satan. Two p.m., your hour
of death, she came to find me – one widow

on her list of grieving widows. Her hands
were thick with rings. Strange to me, she wore
ultra-suede trouser suits in pastel
shades. She was tall, old, bony.

I dared not ask about herself but wondered
if she had lost a husband and now found life
in listening to others speak of grief.
She used few words, none I had not heard,

Nor did she ever touch me as if she and I
were human. Yet her method worked.
I served two cups of tea. Then things poured out
that made me see and feel and weep and weep,

This continued through the spring and summer
that first year when I could not bear
to look at sky or see your constant ending.
I began to write these poems then.

The Heliopause

An image hard to grasp – of space unknown,
of solar winds that slow and stop and shock
in their own zone where our sun ends.
We, if there, are lit by only stars.

On your last night you worked on, 'Letter from Satan'.
You wrote of *non-existence. Reverse of image.*
An edge of cell-thin paper which contains
a thought. And you saw – way up,

on earth's flighty rim, a man in clothes
like yours. And left me here to wrestle with
your words – the house itself precarious –
perched in air a year until my words

returned. Then I could write and see and saw
this image of the deep inside the heliopause.

Cliff Walks

Cornwall

That summer – England suffered.
Even on the coast the heat was monstrous.
All week we argued. How far to go?
You chose Tintagel, the legendary birthplace
of King Arthur. We planned a walk from there

to Dog Leg Harbour in Boscastle, reasonable
save for the heat, and that you were not –
yourself. First you baulked against descending
to the town, then at every cliff side path.
You go down yourself if you're so keen.

I paused. But then a woman hurried past
and headed down. She was carrying an infant,
and on her feet – no protection – flip-flops.
Without a word you turned to follow them.
In the cove you sought out shade and sat.

You told me, *You'd better go. Take your swim.*
I didn't know what to think. You loved the breakers.
You'd race towards them, and you'd race them, jumping,
diving, swimming in. That day I swam
through surf alone. And could not tempt you in.

I misread the moment. I watched you watching
the young mother and child, and felt rebuffed.
In fact they were a ruse to keep hidden
that in December you would die. Just walking,
you were drenched with sweat, but it was hot

and we, not old, yet not so young. I see
that then I did not see but duped myself.
I still believed that you would bury me.
You would go on striding through the future
with our daughter. Both of you – inexhaustible.

.

You stopped us near Tintagel's shadowed cove.
There you spoke of Tennyson's King Arthur.
A *naked babe*, he was flung ashore
to rule until, one by one, the knights
of his round table fell, and so he fell.

You talked about the master poem, 'In Memoriam',
a work that took him twenty years to write,
It *gave relief,* he wrote, *against the cold.*
The loss of his young Cambridge friend Hallam
was the crucial death for Tennyson.

As yours would be for me. (For me.) Despite
the torrid heat and mid-day glare, so caught
in history you felt was live – your passion
for it consuming and promiscuous –
you stood in that mad glare and gave a lecture

on the English Elegy. From Thomas Gray
with his reflections in a country churchyard
to Tennyson, whom you quoted with words
that speak especially to me. *No place
that does not breathe / Some gracious memory.*'

Finally you said, 'Let's find the book.'
We were in luck and did. And a tea room
with a sun-protected garden, wrought-iron
tables, a scent of roses, a tea that came
with scones, mixed-berry jam, and Cornish cream.

Together, we read aloud from Tennyson
and wrote our notes. After you were gone
I found an entry you had made that afternoon.
The words were crabbed and hard to read. I could
hardly read them. 'Could it be angina?'

Crete

Another summer. Ten years later. This time
I've come to western Crete – through storm with hail
that kept us circling an hour before landing.
I took a bus across the mountains, caught
a ferry, then a motor boat that, loaded up

with groceries, and sunken, sped full-throttle
– thrilling, frightening – to a hidden cove.
Sea and cliffs of dusty grey-brown rock
owned, apparently, by the shepherd brothers
who built the two tavernas in the inlet.

No roads for cars. Sheep and goats in hundreds.
A perfect place for me and certain others.
You know the type. They're in your letter-poem
'Mediterranean Holiday', pages from
a nineteen sixties experientialist –

like the girl I was, but not me really.
Everywhere I went, I carried my typewriter,
a Traveller Olivetti, and I wrote reams.
Of course I discoed too and slept off
'exertions'. But I sickened from the freedom.

Too much licence in those days. Now things
feel different. Inside the new – the recognised,
Inevitably the years come with us. Each morning
here I find myself amazed that I can climb
and climb high up. I may be heady but not

reckless. I plan my route with options, try
to set out early, take water. Today I'm crossing
goat-tracks to a ledge of slab that juts
above the gorge. High in the walls, in holes,
the eagles raise their young. I think of Whitman's

eagles and of Tennyson's – the dalliance,
the beating wings, the fall. Looking out for parents
with fresh kill, I think of you. I wonder if
that month you spent in Greece you trekked around
these parts. Hippies came here in the sixties.

I keep hearing stories about those days,
and about the war. In nineteen forty one
the Germans captured Crete. Allied soldiers
brought by ship to Souda Bay near Hania
escaped on foot with no supplies. They crossed

these mountains. The heat. The dust. The lack
of water. How did any one survive?
Two hours here and I'm done in completely.
Not my day for seeing eagles. I rinse
my mouth, wet my head and neckerchief,

– odd amulet, your old cowboy neckerchief–
and stand a minute wondering: Where from here?
I'm picturing the gorge path with its spill
of boulders and different colour markers for paths
that merge, diverge, and for a while, vanish.

It's thrilling but demands full focus step-by-step.
Undecided, I'm locked in thought when something
passing shakes me. Heart thudding, I stop myself
from falling and turn full circle to see nothing
but vast empty sky. I'm suddenly anxious

with a fear beyond all sense, lost
in feelings from the start of this existence.
The first year you were gone, I couldn't look up.
Couldn't bear to see the sky. I felt too small
and unprotected then. How could I live?

Now I chose the gorge path. On the way
I watched a black-haired goat command a branch
so thin, it trembled when he leaped to land.
Yet he walked along it unperturbed,
and stopped as if the air itself could hold him.

A spirit not a spirit – he peed, was gone.
The gorge path ends at Marble (Marmara) Beach.
There I learned a pair of eagles thundered
from the cliff. They soared –suspended – an instant,
then dropped like bullets and sped out to sea.

Heart

Embrace, if you can, the not-yet.
       Geoffrey Adkins,
          'Visit to a London Heart Specialist'

Of course it has come to this. Hurrying
from train to bus inside a city station,
sweating in my coat,

I'm caught and held. Held close, I hear,
long unheard, the soft familiar murmur
of a living heart.

I'm so confounded, I lose myself to listening.
I hear the heart against my ear and hear
your heart beat cease.

This pause is ours. Between the beat and silence,
we can live. But now the murmur drums
a louder lub-dub beat.

This demands a lullaby for grief.
For grief, it beats – beats beyond the grief.

Threads

The mind calms itself with a caress of
images – that over, over, over –
companionable, stroke through grey-lit hours,
mostly comforting but sometimes stunning
with surprise of new awakening. The senses

quicken and are charmed by, let's suppose,
a field of saffron crocus with its spicy,
earthy, sweet-and-bitter, hay-like fragrance.
From dawn, a hum. Ahead, a life in silks
that slide against the body like cool hands.

For her pleasure, Cleopatra's handmaids
rubbed her limbs with saffron-scented oils.
In her bath – red threads of saffron stigmas.
These are riches. Words. The taste of tongues.
A name is ointment in the 'Song of Songs'